WITHDRAWN

Y0-AUI-892

j340.023
G621
W

7414525

CHEROKEE

**Memphis and Shelby County Public Library and Information Center**

For the Residents
of
Memphis and Shelby County

# What Can She Be?
# A LAWYER

# What Can She Be?
# A LAWYER

Gloria and Esther Goldreich
photographs by Robert Ipcar

Lothrop, Lee & Shepard Co. / New York

## ACKNOWLEDGEMENTS

The authors wish to thank the Honorable Leon Becker, Judge of the Criminal Court of the City of New York and Mr. Ralph Hittman, Director of the Boys' Brotherhood Republic of New York for their cooperation. Canon Number 28 of the New York State Bar Association Canon of Professional Ethics prevents the authors from thanking the many attorneys who advised them in the preparation of the text.

*Books in this Series*
What Can She Be? A Lawyer
What Can She Be? A Veterinarian

Copyright © 1973 by Gloria Goldreich, Esther Goldreich, and Robert Ipcar. All rights reserved. No part of this book may be reproduced or utilized in any form or by any means, electronic or mechanical, including photocopying, recording or by any information storage and retrieval system, without permission in writing from the Publisher. Inquiries should be addressed to Lothrop, Lee & Shepard Co., 105 Madison Ave., New York, N.Y. 10016. Printed in the United States of America.

Goldreich, Gloria.
   What can she be? A lawyer.
   SUMMARY: Describes the varied daily activities of Ellen Green, mother and lawyer, who helps people with all kinds of legal problems.
   1. Women lawyers—United States—Juvenile literature. [1. Women lawyers. 2. Lawyers]   I. Goldreich, Esther, joint author.   II. Ipcar, Robert, illus.   III. Title.
KF299.W6G65               340'.023               72-10587
ISBN 0-688-41521-0
ISBN 0-688-51521-5 (lib. bdg.)

For our cousin Jane Ruth

This is Ellen Green. Ellen is a lawyer—an attorney. People come to her when they have legal problems—problems and questions about laws. Laws are rules that protect the rights of people. There are laws that people must obey when they buy or sell a house or business. Other laws tell people what they must do if they want to adopt a child or if they feel they have been cheated. Ellen knows how to help people with their legal problems because she went to law school and then passed an examination.

Mornings are a busy time for Ellen and her family. Before Ellen's husband George leaves for his office, they have breakfast together. Then Ellen starts her work.

Most lawyers work in an office, but Ellen works at home. Working at home gives her a chance to spend a lot of time with her son David. David is proud to have a mother with two jobs. He says, "My mother is a mommy *and* a lawyer!"

Early in the morning Ellen talks on the phone to her clients—the people she is helping and advising. Some lawyers work only with businessmen. Other lawyers work only with large companies.

But Ellen works with all kinds of people and all kinds of problems. Each morning, after Ellen has decided how she can best help her clients, she and David go out together.

David goes to his morning play group and Ellen goes to a special library where all the books are law books. There are so many laws that even lawyers cannot remember them all.

At the law library, Ellen studies the law books that contain cases like those of her clients. Each case in a law book describes a special problem and tells how it was solved. Ellen spends many hours studying cases in order to learn how best to help her clients.

Today she is trying to help an old man named Mr. Philips. For many years Mr. Philips has worked for a company. Now the company has told him that he is too old and must leave his job. Mr. Philips is very upset. He is worried about not having any money.

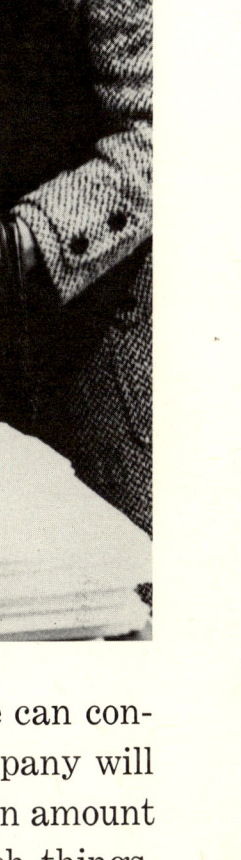

Ellen is trying to find a law that says that he can continue to work. If he cannot, perhaps the company will pay him a pension so that he will have a certain amount of money each month. Laws often decide such things. Ellen finds out that Mr. Philips' company once signed an agreement that says that it must pay its workers a pension when they are too old to work. After he has signed some papers, Mr. Philips can receive his money.

After David's play group, Ellen and David bring the papers to Mr. Philips' office. Ellen explains them and tells him to read them carefully. Mr. Philips is sad to leave his job but happy to know that he will have enough money to buy food and pay his rent. Ellen is glad she was able to help him.

Jimmy Chen has come to see Ellen because his back has been hurt in an automobile accident. Jimmy teaches a special Chinese dragon dance but because he is hurt he cannot teach. Until he is better, Jimmy will have no way to earn money.

He thinks the driver of the car that hurt him should pay him some money because it is his fault that Jimmy cannot work.

Ellen collects evidence—facts that show whether or not Jimmy is telling the truth. She studies photographs of the accident. She talks to someone who was with Jimmy when the accident happened. She is now sure that what Jimmy has told her is true.

She and Jimmy meet with another lawyer who is advising the driver. They talk and agree on the amount of money Jimmy will receive. Cases like this are often decided between two lawyers. When cases can be settled in such a simple, friendly way, the lawyers are glad. Jimmy Chen is pleased that, with Ellen's help, he has won his case.

Not all cases are so simple. Joe Morales has bought a grocery store from a man who promised to leave some display cases in the store. But all the cases were removed. To get the display cases, Joe must sue the man—take him to court. Ellen will represent Joe Morales and speak for him in court.

Ellen presents the case before a judge in a courtroom. She shows the contracts that Joe Morales signed before he bought the store. The lawyer for the man who promised to leave the display cases presents his case. The judge listens carefully. People show respect for judges because it is their job to keep things fair and orderly. When a judge enters or leaves the courtroom, everyone stands. When a judge raps the gavel, everyone is quiet.

The judge who hears Joe Morales' case sees that the contract Mr. Morales has signed does not say exactly *how many* display cases should remain in the store. He decides that Joe will receive only half the number of display cases he wanted. Mr. Morales is disappointed but he has learned a lesson. He will be more careful the next time he signs a contract. He will read every word and see exactly what it says.

Sometimes a judge decides who is right or wrong in a case and sometimes a jury does. A jury is made up of twelve people who have promised to listen carefully to all the evidence and arguments, and to vote fairly for what they think is right.

One of the things Ellen likes about her work is that each day is different. Today Ellen and David visit an old tenement building. When the owner of the building died, a judge asked Ellen to manage it. It is Ellen's job to see that the building is kept in good condition—that it is clean and that the tenants receive enough heat and other services.

23

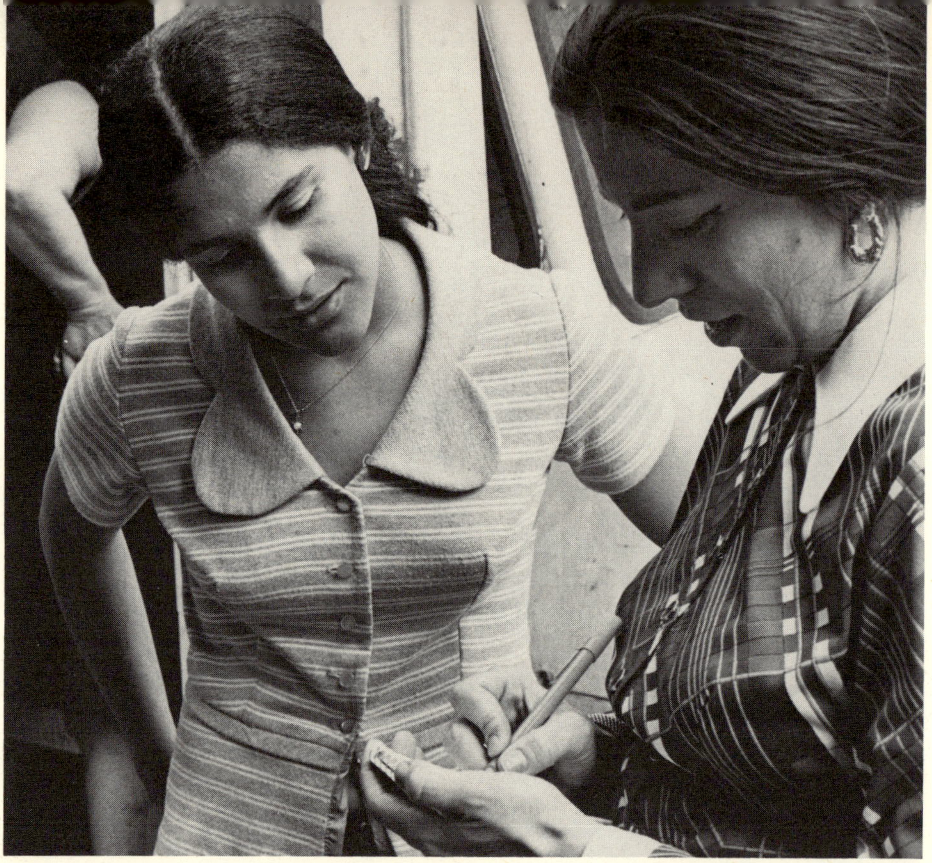

A girl tells Ellen that her family's bathtub must be repaired. A man complains about a dark hallway. A family is moving and Ellen must find a new tenant for the apartment. Ellen listens carefully and asks the superintendent to be sure to take care of everything. She collects the rent and puts it in a special bank account. The money is used to keep the building clean, well-lit, and well-heated.

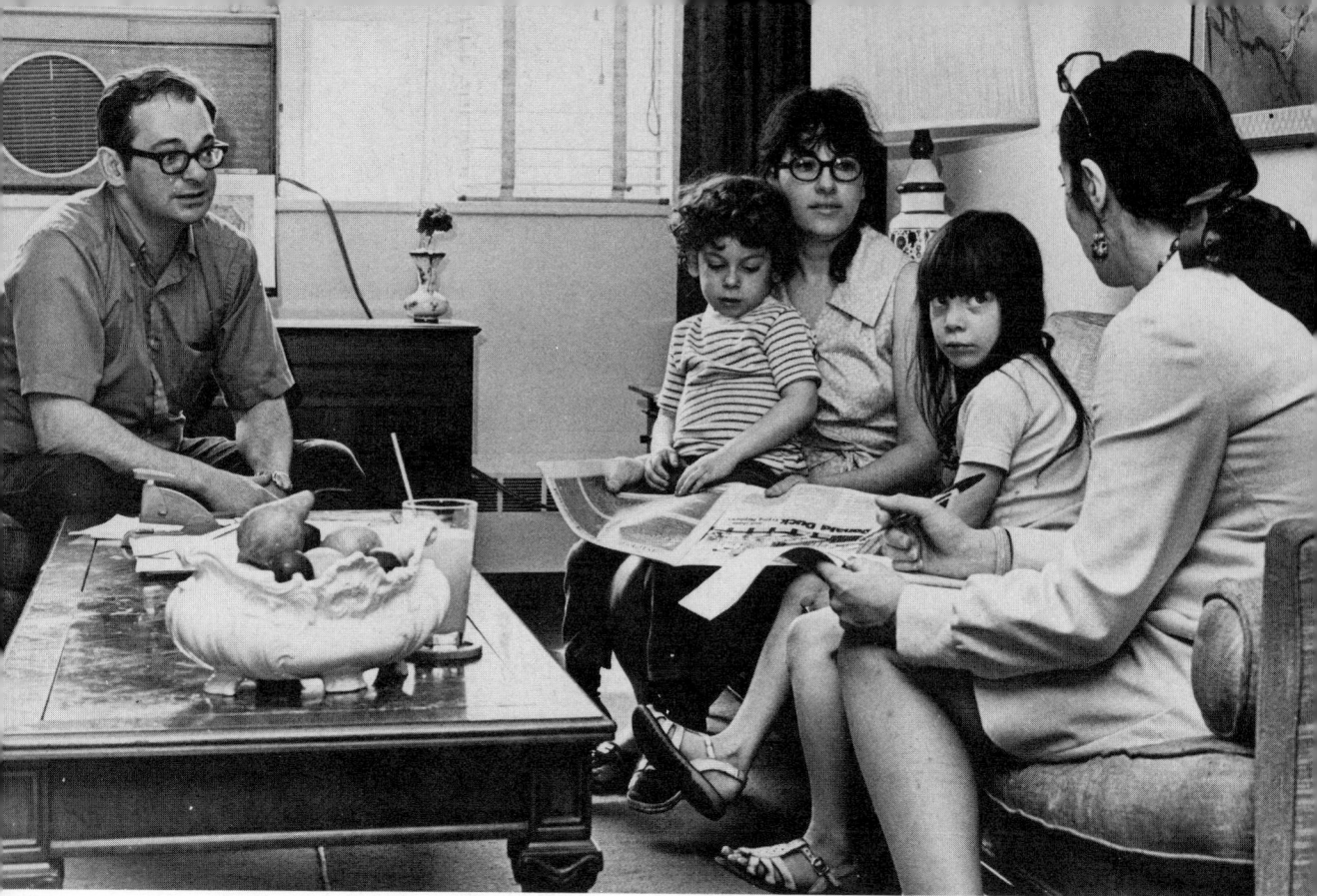

Some days a lawyer's life is very exciting. One day there is a knock at Ellen's door. The Forman family is very upset. They have just received a letter from their landlord telling them they must move out of their apartment immediately. They are being evicted. "What can we do? Where will we sleep?" Mrs. Forman asks. Jolie Forman is crying.

Ellen reads the letter and the papers Mr. Forman shows her. The Formans have refused to pay their rent because their landlord did not fix their broken boiler.

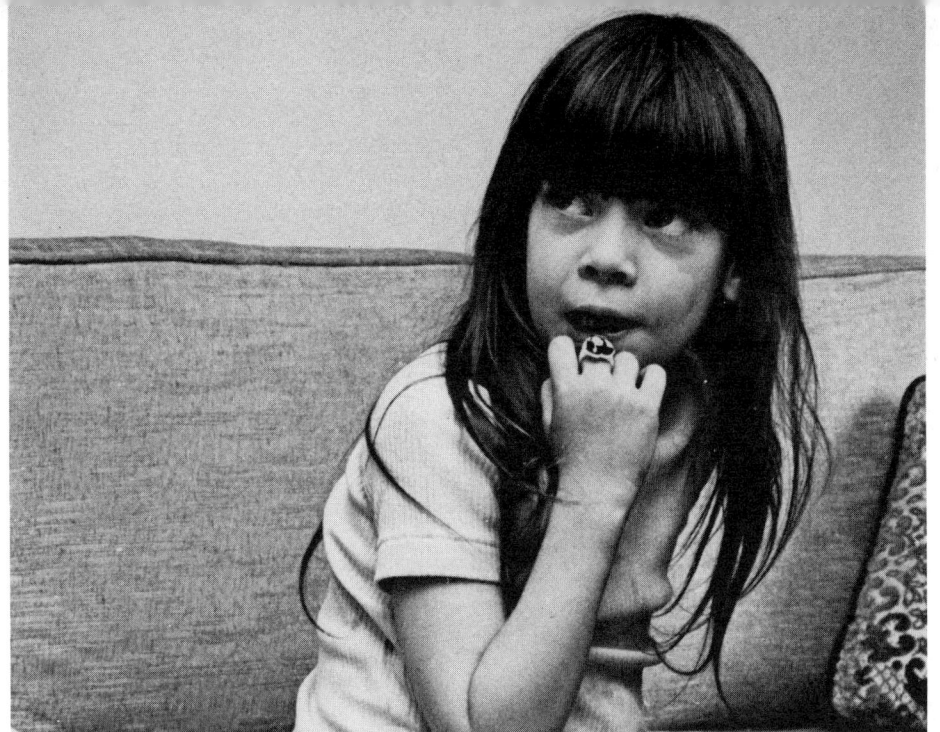

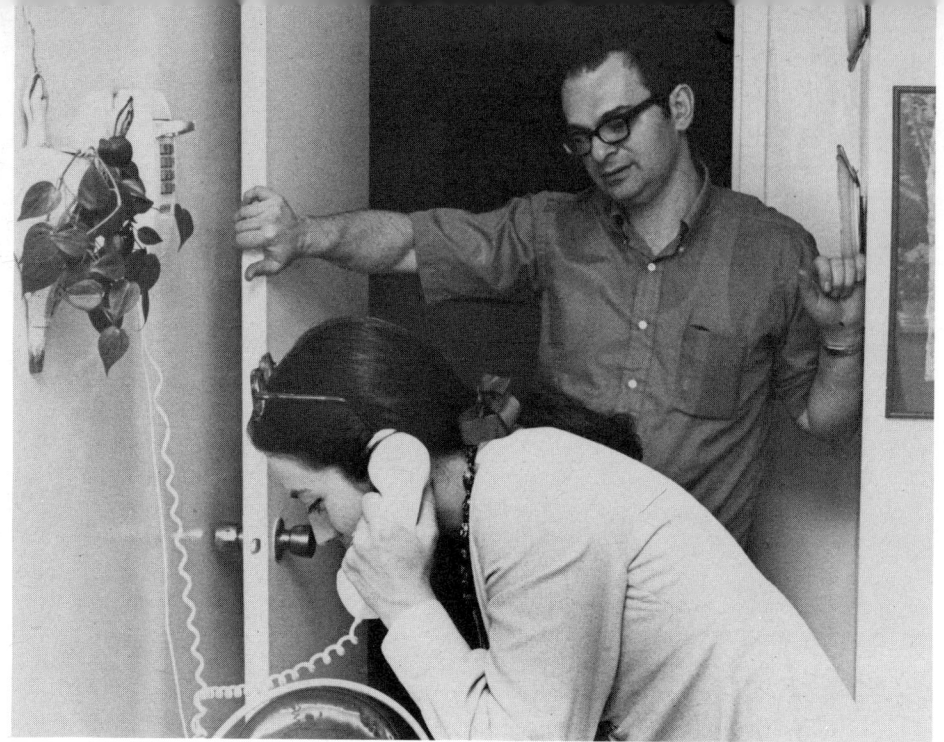

Ellen quickly calls a woman at the Housing Authority and explains everything. "I can help you," the woman tells her, "but you must hurry. It is almost time to close the office."

Ellen dashes into a taxi. When she returns she is smiling.

The Housing Authority has said that if the Formans sign an agreement, they won't have to move. The landlord agrees to fix the boiler and the Formans agree to pay their rent. Everyone is relieved and happy.

An old woman named Mrs. Graham has called Ellen. Mrs. Graham owns an apartment house. She hired a painter who used lead paint and did not do a good job. Lead paint is dangerous and can make little children sick if they accidentally eat it. Now Mrs. Graham must have the house repainted.

Since it was the painter's fault, she doesn't think she should pay for the second painting. Ellen examines the apartment and talks to Mrs. Graham. She will try to help her.

Today David and his mother are going to a very special birthday party. Jennifer Raymond is three years old. Only yesterday the last papers were signed saying that Mr. and Mrs. Raymond were Jennifer's legal parents. They have adopted Jennifer.

There are many children like Jennifer who are adopted by loving parents. Lawyers like Ellen make sure that all the papers are in order and that adopted children belong to their new families forever and ever.

Today at Jennifer's party, everyone is happy. Mr. and Mrs. Raymond are happy because no one can ever take Jennifer away from them. She is part of their family just as though she had been born into it. Jennifer is happy because she has so many birthday presents. Ellen is happy because she helped the Raymonds adopt Jennifer, and David is happy because he loves birthday cake.

Ellen often enjoys talking with her friend Nora, who spends time in the evenings helping poor people who have legal problems. Nora tells Ellen about an article on a new law that she has just read. Lawyers read many books and articles.

Ellen and Nora think one of the most exciting things about their work is that laws are constantly changing and lawyers can help to change them, and make even better and fairer ones.

Sometimes, long after David is asleep, his mother and father are awake and together. Ellen is working. There is always so much to do.

Ellen became a lawyer because she wanted to earn her living doing something that would help people, and make the world a better place to live in. She is proud of what she does. She thinks being a lawyer is the very best kind of work for her.